SandCastle

Word Families Set 4

-um as in drum

Nancy Tuminelly

Consulting Editor Monica Marx, M.A./Reading Specialist

ABDO Publishing Company

Published by SandCastle™, an imprint of ABDO Publishing Company, 4940 Viking Drive, Edina, Minnesota 55435.

Printed in the United States.

Credits
Edited by: Pam Price
Curriculum Coordinator: Nancy Tuminelly
Cover and Interior Design and Production: Mighty Media
Photo Credits: Comstock, Corbis Images, Hemera, Image Source Limited, Photodisc, Rubberball Productions

Library of Congress Cataloging-in-Publication Data

Tuminelly, Nancy, 1952-
        -um as in drum / Nancy Tuminelly ; consulting editor, Monica Marx.
        p. cm. -- (Word families. Set IV)
        Summary: Introduces, in brief text and illustrations, the use of the letter combination
    "um" in such words as "drum," "chum," "hum," and "scum."
        ISBN 1-59197-244-2
        1. Readers (Primary) [1. Vocabulary. 2. Reading.] I. Marx, Monica. II. Title.

PE1119 .T8368 2003
428.1--dc21   2002037910

SandCastle™ books are created by a professional team of educators, reading specialists, and content developers around five essential components that include phonemic awareness, phonics, vocabulary, text comprehension, and fluency. All books are written, reviewed, and leveled for guided reading, early intervention reading, and Accelerated Reader® programs and designed for use in shared, guided, and independent reading and writing activities to support a balanced approach to literacy instruction.

Let Us Know

After reading the book, SandCastle would like you to tell us your stories about reading. What is your favorite page? Was there something hard that you needed help with? Share the ups and downs of learning to read. We want to hear from you! To get posted on the ABDO Publishing Company Web site, send us e-mail at:

sandcastle@abdopub.com

SandCastle Level: Transitional

-um Words

chum

drum

glum

gum

strum

yum

Amy is Mary's chum.

Andy beats the big
drum.

Rob is feeling a bit
glum today.

Cindy blows a bubble
with her gum.

Dan likes to **strum** his guitar.

Joy and her mom eat cake. Yum!

The Chums Who Strum

Tina has a chum.

They both like to strum.

Tina's dad is a beach bum.

He's the one
who taught her to strum.

Sometimes his chum
plays a drum.

When Tina and her
chum would strum,

their friend Nan
would chew gum.

Jan would dance

and Terry would hum.

They are not glum

when Tina and her
chum strum.

Tina even likes to strum

while her dad grills burgers.
Yum! Yum! Yum!

The -um Word Family

bum	mum
chum	plum
drum	scum
glum	strum
gum	sum
hum	yum

Glossary

Some of the words in this list may have more than one meaning. The meaning listed here reflects the way the word is used in the book.

chum a close friend or buddy

glum sad or depressed

hum to sing without moving your lips or using words

strum to stroke the strings of a guitar with your fingers

About SandCastle™

A professional team of educators, reading specialists, and content developers created the SandCastle™ series to support young readers as they develop reading skills and strategies and increase their general knowledge. The SandCastle™ series has four levels that correspond to early literacy development in young children. The levels are provided to help teachers and parents select the appropriate books for young readers.

Emerging Readers
(no flags)

Beginning Readers
(1 flag)

Transitional Readers
(2 flags)

Fluent Readers
(3 flags)

These levels are meant only as a guide. All levels are subject to change.

To see a complete list of SandCastle™ books and other nonfiction titles from ABDO Publishing Company, visit **www.abdopub.com** or contact us at:

4940 Viking Drive, Edina, Minnesota 55435 • 1-800-800-1312 • fax: 1-952-831-1632